Gourmet Romance

Creative ideas for romantic gifts, surprises and experiences

by
MacKenzie and Doug Freeman

Self-help / Relationships

Published by:
Ideascape, Inc.
P.O. Box 1966
Lake Oswego, OR 97035
info@ideascapeinc.com

Distributed by:
Imaginexxus LLC
United States of America

ISBN 0-9655287-0-7

Library of Congress Catalog Card Number:
96-79568

Table of Contents

Dedicated to all expert romantics
and romantics-in-training.

Introduction

Top chefs always look for new recipes for luscious meals. Great romantics are the same way; only they search for creative ways to express their love.

Gourmet Romance is a collection of ideas for gifts, surprises and experiences that can help you create a feast of intimate moments and lasting memories. These romantic recipes include suggested ingredients and preparation instructions. Some recipes may require variations, based on where you live and personal taste.

A ≈ symbol appears at the end of several recipes. The information that follows it is simply a helpful recommendation or suggestion.

This book also contains dozens of special tips plus a section titled *A Dash of Hints*. These tips and hints are useful to everyone, especially romantics-in-training or those who are romantically challenged.

To locate particular recipes, review the *Romantic Recipe Index* at the end. The index rates recipes by cost and complexity.

Enjoy a taste of romance every day. *Gourmet Romance* makes it easy to select and prepare the perfect recipe for romance.

Tempting Gifts & Surprises

A Toast to Us

2   crystal champagne glasses
1   bottle of champagne or sparkling cider
1   gift box or gift bag
1   roll of tissue paper

Celebrate your love.

On a special day or for no occasion at all, wrap up two glasses and a bottle of your favorite sparkling beverage. Give the present to your loved one. Make a toast to your love.

❧ Use one of the following loving toasts or find a book on toasts in the library.

> A toast to love and laughter
> And happily ever after.
>
> Let's drink to love,
> Which is nothing —
> Unless it is divided by two.
>
> Because I love you truly,
> Because you love me, too,
> My very greatest happiness
> Is sharing life with you.

Cater to Your Sweetheart

1   gourmet cooking class on television, through a
     community college or at a specialty market
1   bouquet of flowers
2   candles
2   candleholders
1   book of matches
Ingredients for your gourmet meal
Your finest linens and dishes

It's said that good food is a way to a person's heart.
Select a gourmet cooking class that features your
loved one's favorite foods. Learn how to prepare an
entire gourmet meal.

On the day you plan to serve this special meal, ask a
friend to take your loved one out for the afternoon.
This or another diversion should give you the
necessary preparation time.

Purchase the ingredients for your gourmet meal and
prepare the food.

Set the table with your finest linens and dishes. Add
the romantic touches of flowers and candles. Then
enjoy a special evening together sharing your
handiwork from the kitchen.

Every Day Is a Holiday With You

Your loved one's Christmas or Chanukah stocking
Special gifts

One spring or summer day, hang your loved one's
Christmas or Chanukah stocking by the fireplace.
Place gifts in the stocking, such as a CD, tickets to
an event, candy, jewelry, cologne or lingerie. The
stocking will be the first surprise. Then wait until
your loved one sees what's inside!

❧ Get into the "holiday spirit" even more by
hanging some mistletoe above the mantel or in your
home's entryway.

Famous Lover

1   sheet of paper (8 ½ inches x 14 inches)
1   pen
1   piece of ribbon (6 to 10 inches long)
1   bag of concrete mix (contains cement,
     aggregate and sand)
1   small cardboard box (size to match space next
     to existing concrete on walkway or driveway)
1   roll of waxed paper
1   metallic or plastic gold star (4 inches or larger)
Water

Just as celebrities are honored with a star on
Hollywood's Walk of Fame, your loved one can
have a personal star on your walkway, patio or
driveway.

Write a proclamation honoring your loved one. The
honor could be for the world's best lover, best
spouse, best kisser or other romantic achievement.
Roll up the proclamation and tie it with the ribbon.

When you both are at home, secretly make
preparations for the tribute. First, remove the top
and bottom of the cardboard box. Place the box
"frame" in the desired location and line it with
waxed paper. Prepare the concrete mix according to
the instructions on the bag. Pour the prepared
concrete mix into the box frame. Add the star on
top.

Grab the proclamation. Tell your loved one to close his or her eyes. Guide him or her outside. Explain that you've prepared a tribute.

After the initial moment of surprise, read the proclamation and have him or her autograph the surface with a stick. When the concrete has hardened, remove the box frame and waxed paper.

If you prefer not to place the star permanently in the ground, try one of the following two methods.

Option 1: Follow the instructions above, with one exception. Do not remove the bottom of the box. Line the entire box with waxed paper. Pour the prepared concrete mix into the cardboard "mold."

Option 2: Use plaster of Paris instead of concrete to make a cast that can be placed in a bookcase. To make a cast, follow the preparation instructions on the plaster of Paris package. Pour prepared plaster into a disposable aluminum foil pie pan or roasting pan instead of a cardboard box. After your ceremony is finished and the plaster has hardened, remove the cast from the pan.

Finding Love in Unexpected Places

2   sheets of paper (8 ½ inches x 11 inches)
1   pair of scissors
1   pen

Imagine how much fun your loved one will have discovering romantic messages hidden around the house.

Cut each sheet of paper into eight equal pieces. Fold each piece in half to make a mini-card. Write a note on each card, such as "I love you" or "I am so lucky to have you in my life."

Hide the cards when your loved one isn't home or has gone to bed. Place a card next to a hairbrush, inside a pocket, inside a cereal box, on the handle of the vacuum cleaner, taped to the television remote control or anywhere your loved one would not expect to find a note.

Option 1: Leave one note a day for two weeks, either in the same location or in different locations.

Option 2: Leave a dozen or more notes around the house for your loved one to discover the next day.

Gifts From My Heart

1   or more gift or department store catalogs
1   smartphone, computer or electronic tablet with
     Wi-Fi access
1   Internet search engine
Special gifts

Surprise packages always bring a smile. Specialty shops and catalog companies will deliver a wonderful variety of gifts to your doorstep.

Decide if you want a gift delivered to your loved one monthly, bimonthly or quarterly for a year. Popular items include coffee, beer, wine, desserts, flowers and potted plants.

Order something your loved one will think is special. Your gifts will be a fun reminder of your love.

Gifts You've Given Me

5   to 10 sheets of white paper (8 ½ inches x 11 inches)

1   sheet of fancy paper (8 ½ inches x 11 inches)

1   large stapler

1   pen

Sentimental romantics enjoy recalling favorite moments of their relationship. Do just that with a *Gifts You've Given Me* booklet.

Fold the sheets of white paper in half (8 ½ inches x 5 ½ inches). Slip the sheets inside one another. Fold the fancy sheet of paper in half and use it as the cover. Staple all of the sheets together in the center.

On the cover, write *Gifts You've Given Me* by … (your name). Inside the booklet, write down memories of some times you have shared together. Describe what the times meant to you, how they touched you or how they changed your life. At the end, write something about how you look forward to sharing many more special times together.

❧ You may want to compose your thoughts on scratch paper or on a computer before writing in your booklet.

Got to Get a Message to You

2 phones
1 voice mail or texting service

Most couples don't work at the same location. However, you still can let your loved one know how much you care even during the middle of the day.

Call him or her. If you reach voice mail or prefer to send a text, leave a brief "I love you" message and say that you were thinking of him or her.

Have I Ever Told You...?

1   blank greeting card and envelope
1   pen
1   postage stamp (optional)

Tell your loved one how much you enjoy his or her special qualities.

Make or buy a blank greeting card. Inside, write about some of your loved one's characteristics that you appreciate. For example, say how much you love the way she makes you laugh, how just the sound of his voice can make you feel good or how he knows the perfect moment for a hug and kiss.

Mail the card or leave it on your loved one's pillow.

Image of Love

1	digital photo of you
1	professional photo service or
1	computer or electronic tablet
1	color laser or ink jet printer
1	sheet of photo quality paper
1	pair of scissors or paper cutter

Every romantic should have a wallet photo of his or her loved one.

Find a photograph of you that's especially good. Take it to a professional service to have a copy printed and trimmed to wallet size.

Another option is to make a wallet-size print yourself. Use your own computer or electronic tablet and a printer with photo quality paper. Then trim the photo to be approximately 2 inches x 3 ¼ inches.

Secretly slip the photo into your loved one's wallet.

Wait for the discovery or create a situation that requires your loved one to look in his or her wallet where the photograph is located.

Just a Touch of Love

Kisses
Caresses
Hugs

When your loved one least expects it, sneak up from behind and kiss him or her on the back of the neck. Add some gentle caresses and a hug or two.

❧ After delivering your touch of love softly say, "There's more where that came from." "This is the first installment." or "I just had to let you know."

Long-distance Kisses

1	tube of lipstick or colored lip balm
1	sheet of white paper
1	pen
2	smartphones

If your loved one is across town or possibly out of town and you want to share a kiss, send a long-distance kiss via your smartphone.

First, apply lipstick or lip balm to your lips. Press your lips to the sheet of paper. Do this once or all over the page. Add a romantic message. Next, take a photo of the piece of paper with your smartphone's camera. Send it to your loved one's smartphone.

Love in Any Language

Foreign language dictionaries
Foreign language phrase books

Learn how to say, "I love you" in another language or even several languages. Below are five examples to get you started. Look for others in foreign language dictionaries or phrase books at your local library or online.

Danish -
Jeg elsker dig (yeh-eye ell-skah dye)

French -
Je t'aime (zheh tem)

German -
Ich liebe dich (eekh lee-bah deekh)

Hawaiian -
Aloha au ia oe (ah-low-ha ahoo ee-ah-oh-ee)

Spanish -
Te amo (tay ah-moh)

❧ These phrases are especially handy if you want to say, "I love you," during a phone conversation or special voice mail message.

Love in Cyberspace

2   smartphones, computers or electronic tablets with Wi-Fi access

Send a quick "I love you" message that your loved one will receive first thing in the morning or during the day. If the message is going to be sent to your home computer or smartphone, write a more elaborate and romantic message!

Warning: Some businesses have regulations against use of office computers for personal e-mails.

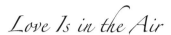

Love Is in the Air

1	helium balloon with a ribbon or string
1	small card and envelope
1	pen

Balloons are a colorful and fun way to express your love.

Buy a helium-filled balloon imprinted with a romantic sentiment or one that is shaped like a heart or lips. Write a love note on the card and attach it to the bottom of the balloon string.

Either tie down the balloon to keep it from floating away or let it rest up against a low ceiling.

❧ If you'd like to add to the surprise, place the balloon in a location where it'll pop out, such as in a car trunk (tied down), closet, cupboard or shower.

♥ ───────────

Lover's Serenade

1   smartphone, computer or electronic tablet with
      Wi-Fi access
1   Internet search engine
Musicians or singers

Just as in the movies, hire some local musicians to
serenade your loved one.

You may find performers through a local high
school or college music department. They also are
listed on the Internet under "Musicians," "Opera
Companies" or "Singing Telegrams."

Position the musicians or singers below a balcony or
outside a large, ground level window to give this
special performance.

❧ Ask a friend to record a video of the serenade
event. Tell him or her to be sure to catch your loved
one's initial reaction.

Morning Shower Surprise

1   big bath towel
1   kiss
1   flower

You typically don't expect anything except a chilly floor after a shower.

One morning, surprise your loved one as he or she steps out of the shower. Give him or her a quick wrap in a big towel, a good morning kiss and a flower. It's a great way to start the day.

Music to Your Ears

1 smartphone, computer or electronic tablet with Wi-Fi access
1 Internet search engine
Music lessons

Learn some of your loved one's favorite songs by taking singing lessons, piano lessons or both.

For listings of music classes or teachers, look online under "Music Instruction." Either perform the medley at home or arrange a performance with a group when you go out for an evening.

☙ If you have stage fright, make a video of your performance. You can send your loved one the video via email or smartphone. Another option is to post it on his or her social network page.

Office Romance

1   small gift
1   card and envelope
1   pen
Delivery service

It's always a nice surprise to receive a gift at work.

Surprise your loved one with flowers, candy or anything special to break up the daily routine. Be sure to write a note so your loved one knows who sent the gift. Consider signing the note, "With love, from Your Secret Admirer."

❧ For added romance, include an invitation for a special rendezvous after work at a designated time and place.

Our Love Story

1   or more new photo or scrap booking album(s)
Photographs of you and your loved one
Small note cards and a pen

Use your favorite photographs to tell your love story.

Select photos of your times together. Arrange them in an album. Place titles at the beginning of each group of photos like chapters in a book. Use titles such as "When We Met" or "The Winter of 2015."

Obtain photos for this album in the following ways:

- Have reprints made of photos in existing albums.
- Use photos currently in a shoebox or drawer.
- Make prints from photos on your computer, electronic tablet or smartphone
- Take new photos with this purpose in mind.

This is a perfect gift for an anniversary or Valentine's Day. However, if you recently met, insert one photograph into the album. Add a note that says you hope to fill the pages with great memories together.

If you have been together for some time and fill up one album, you may want to give an additional album. In a note write, "This blank album is for the second volume of our love story."

Option: If you prefer keeping things digital, create a CD, DVD or a USB flash drive of favorite times together. Place the photos in chronological order or by themes. Be sure to label it with a permanent marker.

Our Song

1   recording of "your song"
1   record player, CD player, MP3 player, computer or electronic tablet

Many couples have a favorite song, one that reminds them of their relationship or a special time together.

Buy a CD or download your song onto your MP3 player, smartphone, computer or electronic tablet.

Part way through dinner, turn on the music and ask your loved one to dance. Your living room or dining room can be your own private dance floor.

Surprise your loved one with this gift another way by slipping the CD into the car stereo, emailing the music file or turning on the MP3 Player. Watch for a smile.

❧ When you're at a restaurant with live or recorded music, ask a band or disc jockey to play your song and invite your loved one to dance.

Passion's Puzzle

1 blank puzzle card
1 envelope
1 pen
Messenger service (optional)

Romance doesn't have to be puzzling. However, a good puzzle can add fun to your relationship.

Write a passion-filled love letter on a puzzle card. These cards often are heart-shaped. They may be purchased in arts and crafts stores or stationery shops.

After you write the letter, disassemble the puzzle and enclose the pieces in the envelope. Personally deliver the envelope to your loved one or have it delivered by mail or a messenger service.

When your loved one opens the envelope, he or she will have fun assembling the puzzle card and reading your passionate prose.

Picture Perfect Romance

1	photo of you and your loved one together
1	photo frame
1	professional photo service or
1	computer or electronic tablet
1	color laser or ink jet printer
1	sheet of photo quality paper
1	pair of scissors or paper cutter

A photo of a special moment together is a wonderful romantic keepsake.

Select a favorite photograph of you and your loved one together. Make a re-print with your computer or electronic tablet and printer using photo quality paper. Another option is to have an enlargement made professionally.

Have the photo trimmed to fit in a unique or exquisite frame.

Coordinate with a co-worker to place the photograph on your loved one's desk for a surprise. If you want to present the photo at home, place it on a table in your living room or bedroom.

Poetic Love

1   sheet of stationery
1   pen

Share some poetic thoughts with your loved one. Write a love poem for him or her. Select from a number of styles, such as one of the following:

Haiku - a non-rhyming poem that has five syllables in the first and third lines and seven syllables in the second line.

Rhyming or non-rhyming - a poem of one or more stanzas where the last word in each line may or may not rhyme.

Limerick - a poem with five lines. Lines one, two and five rhyme and have eight or nine syllables. Lines three and four rhyme and have five or six syllables. Limericks often start with a phrase like, "There once was a man named … "

❧ If poetry is not your strong suit, find a library book on romantic poetry. Use a poem that you like as a guide for inserting your own words.

Postcards From Romanceland

6   postcards
6   postcard stamps
1   special card and envelope
1   pen

Love letters are the lifeblood of hopeless romantics.

Starting on Saturday, write and mail a postcard to your loved one every day for six days. Each day during the next week, he or she will receive a postcard with your message of love.

Then on the second Sunday, slip outside to ring the front doorbell. Personally deliver the last love mail. This may be a love letter or an invitation to do something romantic together that day.

Romantic Boudoir

1   new set of sheets and pillowcases
1   new comforter

Add some romantic touches to your bedroom. An easy way to do this is with new bedding. You can have the luxurious feeling of satin or give your bedroom a theme with a print.

Make your bed with the new bedding. Then invite your loved one into the bedroom for the surprise.

Room for Romance

Fire in the fireplace
Lots of pillows
Romantic music
Appetizers
1   negligee or pair of silk pajamas
1   blindfold

Create a romantic atmosphere at home.

Build a fire in the fireplace and arrange the pillows
in front of it. Turn on some romantic music. Prepare
a few appetizers. Slip into something comfortable.
Blindfold and escort your loved one to your
romantic room. Take off the blindfold and enjoy the
evening together.

Scent-uous Reminder

Your cologne

Say, "I love you!" without saying a word.

Before leaving in the morning, spray some of your cologne into your loved one's car. He or she will think about you on the drive to work or while doing errands.

Secret Love Letter

1 sheet of scratch paper
1 felt tip pen (water-based ink)
1 piece of waxed paper (8 ½ inches x 12 inches)
1 pair of scissors
1 sheet of white paper (8 ½ inches x 11 inches)
1 envelope

Write a letter that truly is "a reflection of your love."

On the scratch paper, compose a brief love letter. Trim the piece of waxed paper to 8 ½ inches x 11 inches.

Take the felt tip pen and copy the letter onto the waxed paper. Gently lay the white sheet of paper on top of the waxed paper. Place one finger at the top of the page to keep the sheets from slipping. Next, with the side of your other hand, stroke across the white sheet in one direction all the way down the page. Remove the white sheet. Now the writing is printed backwards on that sheet.

On the envelope, tell your loved one that this letter can be read only when viewed in front of a mirror.

❧ Some felt tip pens may write better than others on waxed paper. Occasionally, you may have to rewrite some words on the waxed paper.

Tell the World You're in Love

1	smartphone, computer or electronic tablet with Wi-Fi access
1	Internet search engine
1	romantic message

Publicly profess your love so your loved one and the world know how you feel.

Look online for ideas on how to do this. Options include a radio announcement, skywriting message, banner trailing from an airplane, billboard, electronic scoreboard message at a sports event, local magazine or newspaper ad.

After the announcement is scheduled, make the necessary arrangements to have your loved one see or hear it.

❧ Have a friend or relative secretly photograph or record the "live" announcement.

The Spy Who Loves You

3   or more magazines or newspapers
1   pair of scissors
1   sheet of paper (8 ½ inches x 11 inches)
1   glue stick
2   envelopes
1   postage stamp
1   smartphone
1   voice memo app
1   public meeting place
1   "spy" disguise or costume

Is there enough intrigue in your romance? Try using some spy tactics.

Cut out a variety of letters from several magazines or newspapers. Using the cutout letters and paper, glue together a message that looks like a note from a spy. The message should indicate that a spy has some romantic secrets to disclose and that your loved will receive further instructions. Put the note inside an envelope and mail it to your loved one.

With your phone, record detailed instructions using an app that records memos. Try altering your voice. State when and where your loved one should go to meet this spy, perhaps at a restaurant, café or pub. Say that he or she should look for someone dressed in a trench coat, hat and wearing a red carnation.

You may substitute another disguise. The key is to be recognizable as the spy, but not necessarily as yourself. Also say on the recording that your loved one should approach the spy cautiously and whisper a specific romantic code.

Send the voice memo to your loved one's smartphone with the subject line: "Listen now for further instructions."

As the clandestine meeting progresses, discuss some romantic secrets and enjoy the intrigue. Then take it from there. Good spies always know what to do next.

Warning: Do not leave messages that would alarm your loved one. Be sure to make the messages suspicious, but obviously made in fun.

Time for Us

1   clock or watch
1   card and envelope
1   pen

True love lasts forever.

The gift of a beautiful timepiece will symbolize your love. Attach a card with a sentiment referring to time. Some ideas are: "Forever together," "For all time" or "I love every minute I spend with you."

❧ Have the timepiece engraved with your sentiment. Engraving may be offered at the gift shop or jewelry store where you purchased the gift.

Trail of Hugs and Kisses

12 or more gift tags or small blank cards
1 pen
1 card and envelope (optional)
Wrapped candies, flower petals or confetti

Blaze a romantic trail marked by hugs and kisses.

Make a dozen or more hug and kiss coupons by writing "One Hug" or "One Kiss" on each tag or card. Create a trail using wrapped candies, flower petals, confetti or other colorful items. Start from the garage or front door. Leave a hug or kiss coupon every few yards along the trail. Continue through the house to your bedroom and onto your bed.

Wait in the bedroom as your loved one follows the trail through the house. When he or she arrives there, explain that the coupons are redeemable immediately or over time. If you can't be home, leave a love note at the end of the trail that mentions when the coupons may be redeemed.

After this trek, lots of hugs and kisses are a well-earned reward.

Treat for My Sweet

Your loved one's favorite food or drink
1   small card and envelope
1   pen

A surprise treat is a wonderful pick-me-up. This may
be a food or drink that your loved one rarely gets
because of the expense, availability or calories. Live
it up — a special treat shows that you are thinking of
him or her.

How you deliver the treat depends on what it is.
You could place it in your loved one's briefcase,
purse, lunch sack, on the car dashboard or in a
prominent location in the refrigerator. Always attach
a note expressing a loving thought.

Twelve Times the Romance

1   rose or favorite flower every month

Show your loved one that you remember the day you met or were married by giving him or her a flower on that day every month. This gives you an opportunity to celebrate your love throughout the year.

Note: If you met or were married on the 29th, 30th or 31st, there will be one to five months when you may have to substitute either the last or first day of the month to celebrate.

❧ Ask a florist or check a book at the library or online to learn the special meanings of flowers. Here are a few examples:

Blue Violet ....Faithfulness
Bridal Rose ....Happy love
Spanish Jasmine.....................Sensuality
Variegated Tulip ....Beautiful eyes
White Lily.........................…Sweetness

Ultimate Indulgence

1   smartphone, computer or electronic tablet with Wi-Fi access
1   Internet search engine
1   reservation for dinner and dancing
1   appointment with a professional photographer
Appointments with personal care professionals

Surprise your loved one with a day of pampering. Services may include a massage, manicure, pedicure, facial, hairstyling or wardrobe consultation. Afterwards, take him or her to a professional photographer's studio for a photo session. To choose the services you want, look online for local listings under "Barbers," "Beauty," "Color Consultants," "Massage" or "Photographers." Finish the day with a night on the town to celebrate his or her new look.

Video Lovegram

1   smartphone, electronic tablet or video camera
1   blank DVD or USB flash drive
1   large envelope
1   pen
Romantic music
Postage (optional)

Secretly record a love letter for your sweetheart. Say or do something to express your love. You could read a letter, recite poetry or just speak informally. Try to create a natural or romantic scene, such as with you sitting in a comfortable chair next to the fireplace. Consider adding music to the background.

You could e-mail the recording to your loved one. Another option is to make a DVD or record the file to a USB flash drive, put it in the envelope and address it to your loved one. Either mail the envelope or leave it in a visible location with the message "Open Me" on the front.

What's for Dinner?

1   smartphone, computer or electronic tablet with
    Wi-Fi access
1   Internet search engine
3   to 4 restaurant reservations

If there are several restaurants that you and your
loved one have wanted to try, arrange the surprise of
a progressive dinner.

Check the restaurant listings online. Select three or
four restaurants for your date. The first stop will be
for a drink and appetizers. At the second restaurant,
order only a main course. End the evening at an
establishment known for its desserts. If this place
does not have dancing or live music, you might
want to go to a fourth place that does offer music
and serves coffee or drinks.

❧ If possible, choose restaurants that are within
walking distance of each other. This will give you an
opportunity to walk off some calories and stroll arm
in arm.

Whisper Sweet Nothings

1   book of romantic quotes or thoughts
1   book of romantic song lyrics
1   book of romantic lines from movies
1   computer, electronic tablet or smartphone with
      Wi-Fi access
1   Internet search engine

A whispered message of love will make your loved
one smile or blush. Loving words are especially nice
when they are least expected.

Check out library books or do a search online to
find romantic phrases. Select a few choice ones and
memorize them. Wait for the right moment when
you are next to your loved one in the car, at a
theater, at a restaurant, on the couch at home or at a
party. Whisper something affectionate in your loved
one's ear.

Option: If you don't have time to research romantic
phrases, then a simple "I love you" or "I think you're
sexy" will work every time.

Would You Marry Me, Again?

1   sheet of scratch paper
1   pen
1   romantic setting

If you want to make your spouse feel extra special, propose to him or her again.

Write out the words you want to say. Practice the proposal a few times. Choose a time and place that has meaning for both of you. When you make your proposal, it'll be a romantic moment the two of you can relive.

❧ Promise your love to one another again or make plans together to renew your vows.

Epicurean Delights

A Couple of Flirts

1   restaurant, café or bar
2   drinks

Have some fun flirting — with each other.

Either walk separately into a restaurant, café or bar or arrange to meet there. Sit at different tables. Order two drinks and send one over to your loved one's table. Then sit together after it's been delivered and you've flirted across the room.

≈ Flirt even more by including a love note along with the drink you send to your loved one.

Afternoon Delight

2   or more hours
2   lunches
1   hotel reservation (optional)

Arrange your schedules to take either a long lunch hour or the afternoon off. Meet for a leisurely lunch at home. Then let romance take its course. Another option is to have a quick meal at a restaurant and go to a hotel afterwards for some private post-lunch romance.

≈ For a romantic twist, serve lunch in bed if you meet at home. If you go to a hotel, order room service instead of eating at a restaurant.

Amused Romantics

2   or more amusement ride tickets

Life and love are filled with ups and downs. You can share them together, especially at an amusement park, county fair or state fair. Most of these places have a Ferris wheel or roller coaster. Hold hands and share a kiss before, during and after each ride.

An Exclusive Drive-in Theater

1   movie on DVD, Blu-ray or pay-per-view service
1   DVD player, Blu-ray player, laptop computer or
      electronic tablet
1   table (optional)
1   television (optional)
1   car
1   blanket
Assorted refreshments

The next time you want to watch a movie, go to your private drive-in theater.

Rent a movie you both would like to see either from the library, store or pay-per-view service. Try a thriller so you hold each other tightly through the tense scenes. Find a love story to spark a romantic mood. Pick a comedy and laugh together all night.

Set up the equipment in your garage. If you choose to use your television and DVD or Blu-ray player, set them on a table in front of the windshield. Then sit in the car and roll down the windows to hear. However, if you decide to use a laptop computer, electronic tablet or smartphone, make sure that it's fully charged. Then simply set that device on the car's dashboard.

Use the remote control or pause button to stop the movie when you need more refreshments or want tosmooch in the backseat. If you become cold, get closer and share the blanket.

Warning: Never run your car's engine to use the heater while in a closed garage.

Bicycle Built for Two

1   smartphone, computer or electronic tablet with
    Wi-Fi access
1   Internet search engine
1   tandem bicycle
2   cans of your favorite beverage

A tandem bicycle ride is great fun and takes
teamwork. Rent a tandem bicycle for a few hours.
You may find one at a local shop listed online under
"Bicycles Rental."

Peddle around town, on country back roads or in a
park. Bring along something cold to drink to quench
your thirst.

❧ A tandem bicycle ride is particularly enjoyable to
share if you live in or are traveling through an area
noted for its vineyards, fall foliage or spring flowers.

Candlelight Romance

4   or more candles and candleholders
1   book of matches

Romance each other by candlelight.

Instead of turning on the lights one evening, light as many candles as you have candleholders. Spend the entire evening cuddling, reading to one another or talking about your dreams for the future.

At the end of the evening, each of you should blow out half of the candles. Be sure to make a different romantic wish on each candle before blowing it out.

Caught on Film

1   instant photo booth
Photo frame(s)

Get caught in the act of romance.

When the two of you pass by an instant photo booth, pop in. Use a variety of fun poses, such as hugging, kissing or simply being close and happy. Frame some or all of the photos so they can be displayed on a wall, desk or refrigerator door.

Celebrate the Day You Met

1   camera
1   smartphone or electronic tablet
Items used on the day you met

Celebrate the anniversary of the day you met.

Arrange to do the same thing you were doing then or a modification of the activity. Be sure to take photos or record this event every year.

❧ You may wish to do this for the anniversary of your first date, too. You can never celebrate your love too often.

European Sidewalk Café

1   table
1   tablecloth
2   chairs
2   coffee cups
1   espresso maker with fresh coffee
Snacks
French or Italian music
1   electronic tablet, record, CD, MP3 player or
      smartphone

Enjoy an afternoon or evening as if you were dining at a sidewalk café in Paris or Rome.

Place a table with a tablecloth and two chairs in your breakfast nook or on the patio. Add more realism by using café-style furniture, such as wire chairs and a table with an umbrella. Play a recording of some nice café mood music.

Your table for two awaits you.

❧ Go all out and add a lamppost or other props to set the scene. Hire a student studying French or Italian to be your waiter or waitress for a couple of hours.

Giant Fortune Cookies for Romantics

Fortunes

2   sheets of different colored paper (4 inches x 4 inches)

2   pens

1   pair of scissors

2   airtight containers

Fortune Cookie Dough

7 ½ teaspoons of sweet butter

2   large egg whites

½   cup of sugar

½   cup of all-purpose flour, sifted

4 ½ teaspoons of heavy cream

½   teaspoon of almond extract

Nonstick cooking spray

Writing Your Fortunes

Be your own fortune-tellers with personalized fortune cookies.

Each of you selects one sheet of paper and cuts it into four, 1 inch x 4 inches pieces. Secretly write four romantic fortunes for each other. Fold the fortunes in half lengthwise.

Making the Fortune Cookies

In a small saucepan, melt the butter over low heat. Set aside.

Combine egg whites and sugar in a small bowl. Beat with an electric mixer on medium speed for 30 seconds. Add flour and beat until smooth. Add melted butter, heavy cream and almond extract. Beat for 30 seconds until combined.

Coat a cookie sheet with nonstick cooking spray.

Drop 1 tablespoon of batter onto half of the baking sheet. With the back of a spoon, spread the batter into a thin 5-inch circle. Make a second cookie on the other half of the sheet using the same process.

Bake at 400 degrees Fahrenheit for 8 minutes or until the edges turn golden brown.

Remove the cookies from the oven. Working quickly, place one cookie upside down on a paper towel. Using the towel to protect your fingers, loosely fold the cookie in half like a taco. Gently bend the folded side, in the middle, over the edge of a bowl. Hold for 12 seconds. Place the cookie on a clean kitchen towel.

Repeat this process with the other cookies, remembering to spray the cookie sheet before placing the dough each time.

When the cookies have cooled completely, insert one fortune inside each cookie. Store the cookies in two labeled airtight containers, one for each of you. Open one cookie each after a romantic dinner.

Yield: 8 fortune cookies.

Good Clean Fun

1   bathtub full of warm water
1   packet or bottle of bubble bath
5   or more votive candles and candleholders
1   book of matches
2   champagne glasses
1   bottle of champagne or sparkling cider

Share a relaxing evening with your loved one and piles of bubbles.

As you fill up the bathtub with warm water, add your favorite bubble bath. Light the candles. Turn off the lights and pour two glasses of "the bubbly." Enjoy your romantic tub for two.

❧ Bring two bubble pipes or wands into the tub with you. Have fun blowing giant bubbles or streams of bubbles.

Good Deeds for Love's Sake

1   local newspaper
1   smartphone, computer or electronic tablet with Wi-Fi access
1   Internet search engine
1   community organization or other good cause
1   or more hours of your time and lots of enthusiasm

Volunteer together to help a local community organization, nonprofit agency or other good cause. Select a volunteer activity that you both will enjoy doing.

To find out what's available, look in your newspaper or online for lists of volunteer opportunities or contact a community organization that you support. Parents and non-parents can arrange with some schools to assist with classes, events or serve as speakers on careers. You'll be doing good in your community and experiencing something special together.

Good Morning, Good Night Sweetheart

Local newspaper or online weather site
1   blanket
2   mugs
1   container of hot chocolate, coffee or tea

Nature provides romantic backdrops every day with the sunrise and sunset. Check the newspaper or online site to find out the time of the next day's sunrise or sunset. Decide which you'd like to see.

If you plan to see a sunrise, give yourselves enough time to wake-up and walk, ride or drive to a spot where you'll have a good view. Good view spots include the top of a hill or rooftop of a building with public access. Curl up together with the blanket, pour something to drink and start the morning by enjoying a beautiful sunrise.

If you choose to watch a sunset, you may wish to find a spot that overlooks the ocean, the mountains, river or a lake. This is a romantic way to end any day or start a weekend.

Grab Bag Date

1   sheet of paper (8 ½ inches x 11 inches)
1   pair of scissors
2   pens
2   paper bags

Here is a fun way to decide on a date activity. It's also a great way to learn more about each other's interests.

Cut the paper into 10 pieces. Each of you writes down five different activities to do together. Put the pieces into separate paper bags. With eyes closed, your loved one selects one activity from your bag and you select one activity from his or hers. Then do both activities.

It's Time for Recess

1   park with playground equipment
Sports equipment

It's probably been too long since you've played like kids during recess.

Go to a school playground or park and play on the equipment. Push one another on the swings, play on the merry-go-round, climb around the monkey bars, sit on the teeter-totter and slide on the slide. Note: Make certain the equipment will safely accommodate adults before you use it.

You also might want to take a softball and mitts, football, soccer ball or basketball. Remember, this is not a competition; it's a date just to have fun.

❧ Make up new rules for some games. For example, play tag with the "penalty" for getting caught is a kiss.

Just Because Day

2   sheets of paper (8 ½ inches x 11 inches)
1   pair of scissors
1   pen
2   bowls

Create your own romantic holiday, just because you're together.

To select a date for your "Just Because Day," start by cutting the paper into 43 pieces. Write the names of the months on 12 pieces. Put these pieces into one bowl. Next, write the numbers 1 to 31 on the remaining blank pieces. Put the numbered pieces into the other bowl.

You or your loved one must reach into the first bowl and pick a month. Next, the other person must select a day. The date (day and month) chosen now becomes your Just Because Day. Re-select a date only if the one you picked is a special day that you already celebrate or not an actual date, such as February 31.

Always plan to do something romantic on your Just Because Day.

Lazy Afternoon Together

1   hammock or blanket
2   pillows
Blue sky with some clouds

One lazy afternoon, lie in a hammock together or
spread out a blanket in your backyard or a park.
Bring along two pillows if you want some extra
comfort. Lie side by side and look at the clouds. Use
your imaginations describing the cloud shapes and
make up stories about them. Talk about your dreams
and romance.

Life's Romantic Adventures

1   smartphone, computer or electronic tablet with Wi-Fi access
1   Internet search engine
1   adventure of your choice
1   camera

Experience an adventurous activity that both of you always have wanted to try. Consider activities such as a whitewater raft trip, llama trek in the country, tandem parachute jump or sailplane ride. Check online for local services, tours or a travel agent specializing in travel adventures.

Sharing some thrills or experiencing activities that are out of the ordinary could produce some of your favorite times together. During the adventure, be sure to take photos with a regular camera or the one on your smartphone.

Lingering With Lingerie

1	mail order catalog or store's Web site featuring nightwear
1	smartphone or electronic tablet with Wi-Fi access
2	nightwear garments

Snuggle up together and look through the mail order catalog or store's Web site. Once you find something you both like, order it. Ideally, find one piece of nightwear each.

When your garments are delivered, plan a special romantic evening. The evening could begin with a private fashion show for each other. Then test-wear the garments starting with a passionate kiss and long embrace.

Love Afloat

1   rowboat
2   life jackets
1   book of love poems
Light snacks

Have an old-fashioned date afloat in a rowboat.

Rent a boat if you don't own one. Go to a nearby lake. Take turns rowing, reading romantic poems and feeding one another grapes or snacks.

Option: Rent a leg-powered paddleboat. As you sit side by side, hold hands and sneak an occasional kiss. When you feel like taking a break, float around and read poetry to one another. Sip on a drink, snack on the grapes or just nibble on your loved one's ear.

Love Keeps Growing

1   seedling or small tree
1   bag of potting soil
1   container (optional)
Water

Plant a tree in honor of your love.

Decide if you'll plant the tree outside or place it inside your home. If you choose to plant it outside, try a flowering tree that will blossom each year. If you select an evergreen, you could decorate it for the holidays. A tree indoors could be placed in your bedroom or a location in which you spend a lot of time together.

Go to a garden center. Select a tree you both like. Ask about the proper soil, light, planting and fertilization requirements for the tree.

Both of you should be responsible for taking care of the tree. Watch it grow over the years, just as your love grows.

❧ Commemorate a special day in your relationship by planting a tree.

Love Letters in the Sand

No matter where you live, the two of you can enjoy a day at "the beach."

Option 1:
Access to a beach

Go to the beach. Walk hand in hand along the shore. With a stick write "I LOVE YOU" in the sand next to your initials, such as H + J. Make a sand castle. Sit and watch the waves until sunset.

Option 2:
Newspapers or plastic sheeting
1   50-pound sack of sand
1   CD or electronic download with sounds of the ocean
1   electronic tablet, MP3 player or smartphone
1   wading pool filled with water

Create a beach if you live too far from the ocean. Pour the sand onto the newspapers or plastic sheeting. Turn on the device with the sounds of the ocean. Take off your shoes and sit on the sand. Using your fingers, write love letters to each other in the sand. Then cool off by dangling your feet in the pool.

Magnificent Massage

1   pillow
1   bed or several cushions
1   container of scented oil or lotion
2   or more candles and candleholders
1   book of matches
Romantic music

Enjoy the sensual delight of a loving massage.

Arrange the bed or cushions to provide a comfortable place to lie down. Light the candles. Turn off the lights. Turn on some romantic music and disrobe. Take turns giving each other a gentle back rub. Add some tender kisses along the way.

May I Carry Your Books to School?

1   workshop class schedule from a public parks
    bureau, athletic club, community center or
    college either printed or online
2   course registration forms

One way to keep young at heart and share new
experiences is always to be learning. Couples
typically share common interests, many of which
are never fully explored.

Select a course both of you'd like to take. It could be
anything you think is fun, such as painting, folk
dancing, handwriting analysis, bird watching or
tennis. Choose an interest that you'll continue
pursuing together once the class is finished.

More Time for Romance

1   neighbor or student willing to help for the
     evening

Your home is your castle. One evening, have some fun being treated like royalty.

Rather than doing your typical chores at the end of the day, spend the time with one another. Hire a college student or neighbor to be your butler or maid for an evening. Negotiate a fee based on the tasks that will be performed.

Have dinner prepared by your helper, a caterer or a restaurant take-out service. Ask your helper to set the table, serve the meal and wash the dishes. The key to this evening is for the two of you to relax and enjoy more time together.

Playing Favorites

2   sheets of paper (8 ½ inches x 11 inches)
2   pens

Sample a few of each other's favorite things.

Together, make a list of 10 categories of favorite things. These categories could be anything, such as foods, clothes, movies, television shows, sports, music, plays or vacation spots. Separately, fill in a specific favorite thing for each category.

Agree on three categories and arrange to do, see, wear or experience them as a date. For example, you might end up drinking your two favorite beverages, while watching your two favorite movies, at your (jointly) favorite luxury hotel.

---❤️---

Private Campsite

2   sleeping bags or blankets
2   pillows
2   skewers
2   chocolate bars
1   bag of marshmallows
1   box of graham crackers
1   fireplace with a wood fire
1   romance novel, fairy tale book or another book

Go camping together…indoors. Make s'mores. Tell or read stories to one another. Sleep in front of the fireplace. It's camping. It's romance. Best of all, there are no mosquitoes or ants.

S'mores
Put two marshmallows on a skewer. Roast them over the coals until golden brown. Carefully remove the marshmallows from the skewer. Place the roasted marshmallows and a square of chocolate between two graham cracker squares.

Warning: Do not place sleeping bags, blankets or other flammable items too close to the fireplace. Keep fireplace doors or screens closed for safety.

Quest for the Best

1 small notebook
1 pen
1 smartphone, computer or electronic tablet with Wi-Fi access
1 Internet search engine
1 local map (optional)

You deserve the best together, so go find it.

Together, decide on a type of beverage, appetizer, main course, dessert, snack or other food item that both of you especially enjoy. Specific foods and beverages could include Pinot Noir wines, barbecued ribs, pepperoni pizzas or mocha truffles. Make a list of the local vendors for that food item, including specialty stores, restaurants and pubs.

Go on a search for the best of that favorite food. Record your ratings and comments in the notebook and map or on one of your electronic devices. The process of searching for the best may be as much fun as actually finding the best — and you'll do it together.

ॐ Continue your quest on vacations. There even are special tours coordinated around tasting wines, chocolate and other foods. You may become connoisseurs of your favorite food.

Rendezvous for Two

1	smartphone, computer or electronic tablet with Wi-Fi access
1	Internet search engine
1	local guidebook
1	bed and breakfast reservation service
1	country inn or bed and breakfast reservation

Rather than spend the extra time and money to go out of town, try a getaway in your hometown.

Stay at a local bed and breakfast or country inn near your home. Accommodations may be listed online or in a local guidebook. Make the arrangements yourself or through a reservation service. The quality of bed and breakfast homes and inns vary, so inquire before you book a reservation.

Check in at the earliest time possible. Spend as much time in your room as you like or go sightseeing to places you always have meant to see. Enjoy the area as visitors would. Come back to your room and be pampered in the morning with a gourmet breakfast.

Skating Together
(but Not on Thin Ice)

2   pairs of ice skates, in-line skates or roller skates
1   squirt bottle or hot drink container filled with a
     favorite drink
Protective gear

Skating is a romantic way to spend time together
while getting some exercise. Depending on the type
of skating you'd like to do, go to an ice rink or find
an uncrowded location with a smooth surface.
Paved walking paths, empty parking lots and indoor
facilities all work well.

Try skating while holding each other's hand. If one
of you slips, the other will be there to grab hold.
Share squirts of your favorite drink, without squirting
each other too much. Or if you prefer something
hot, snuggle together as you share the drink. The
experience should provide laughs, love and lots of
fun together.

Starlight, Star Bright

2   cups of hot chocolate, tea or dessert coffee
1   lounge chair or porch swing for two
1   large, warm blanket
Night sky with stars
Romantic music

On a clear night, look at the stars in the sky and in your loved one's eyes. Fix two hot drinks. Place a comfortable chair for two on the deck, patio, lawn or porch. Put on some romantic music. Grab a warm blanket, if necessary. Snuggle in for the evening under a canopy of stars.

Find two stars you like and could identify again. Name your stars in honor of one another. Use your first names, nicknames or possibly made-up names. Make a wish upon your stars.

∾ From time to time throughout the year, point to your stars and share a kiss.

Strolling Together

1   peaceful place to walk
1   café

Select a place where you'd like to take a long, romantic walk. Try a park, beach, country road or forest trail. Walk hand in hand or arm in arm.

Afterwards, stop at a café for something to drink. Continue holding hands, even if you get smiles and giggles from jealous passersby.

❧ For extra romance, take a stroll under a full moon.

Take-out, Make-out

1   park bench in a private location
1   boxed breakfast or lunch for two

Either start or break up your workday with a touch of romance. Plan to meet for breakfast or lunch at a favorite park or rooftop. Share your meal and some kisses.

Option: If it is difficult for one of you to get away, plan an in-office date. However, do not allow any interruptions by the phone or other employees.

---❤---

The Language of Love

1   community college or university course
    schedule
1   smartphone, computer or electronic tablet with
    Wi-Fi access
1   Internet search engine
Course registration

The languages of French, Italian, Portuguese and
Spanish are rich in words of passion. Enroll together
and learn one of the Romance languages. Then
speak to each other in a language of love. Do this
whenever you meet, during phone conversations,
while dancing or before saying good night.

Find out about language courses that are available
by looking in a local community college or
university course schedule. Another resource is
online. Look for listings under "Language Schools."

Option: If you live in a town without a college, there
are still several options available. Possibly someone
in your community is fluent in another language and
would consider teaching you. Another alternative is
with libraries that make language lessons available
on CD to be checked out. These recordings may
also be purchased online from various vendors.

The Malt Shop

1   sundae or banana split
2   spoons

The jukebox may be a thing of the past, but sharing a cool treat is not. Go to an ice-cream parlor or drive-in restaurant. Order one big sundae or banana split. Eat the dessert together or feed one another.

Option: Order one extra large milk shake, malt or soft drink with two straws. Sit side by side so you can be close and share.

———————— ♥ ————————

Trip to Nowhere

2   round trip city bus or train tickets

Pick a city bus or commuter train at random and ride to wherever it's going. If you see an interesting restaurant, shop or activity along the way, get off and enjoy yourselves. Otherwise, ride to the end of the line just for the fun of it. This is a great way to get to know a city and share a romantic adventure.

❧ Take along a few snacks if the ride will be a long one. Also, bring a city or transit map or smartphone so you don't become lost.

♥

Try This on for Size

1   boutique, department store or mall

Go window-shopping together. Take turns picking out some clothing items for each other to try on. Select items you always have wanted to see your loved one dressed in. It is chooser's choice with regard to the store and clothing items; you cannot say no. Afterwards, buy each other one item or just plan another shopping date for later in the year.

❧ This type of date may be helpful as an incentive for someone on a diet.

Turn Back the Clock

Music from your past
Stereo, MP3 player, CD player, electronic tablet or
    smartphone
Fire in the fireplace
Your photos in albums, on CDs or electronic device
1   sheet of paper (8 ½ inches x 11 inches)
1   pen

Spend an evening reminiscing about your times
together.

Turn on the music and sit in front of the fireplace.
Look at photos of your wedding, vacations or other
good times. Make notes about activities or trips
you'd like to schedule again.

Walking in a Winter Wonderland

Snow
Fire in the fireplace
2   cups of hot buttered rums, cocoa, coffee or tea

Just as in the carol *Winter Wonderland*, take a walk in the snow. Build a snowman. Then at home, enjoy a hot drink together. Warm up some more by sitting in front of a fire and holding one another tightly.

❧ Consider naming your snowman Parson Brown, as in the carol. Then exchange or renew your vows in front of this "minister."

Will You Go out With Me?

2 phones
1 dinner reservation
1 small gift (flowers, candy or cologne)

No matter how long you have been together, there's something special about being asked out on a date.

Call your loved one and invite him or her out for a romantic evening. Consider going to a restaurant the two of you have wanted to try. Follow up with a movie or live music in an intimate setting.

When you meet, present your loved one with a bouquet of flowers or another small gift.

Five-star Specialties

---❤---

A Chapter From a Romance Novel

1   smartphone, computer or electronic tablet with
     Wi-Fi access
1   Internet search engine
1   blanket
1   saddlebag filled with picnic food and utensils
Rental of one or two horses

Many romance novels have scenes of lovers riding
horses through the countryside, then sharing a
picnic and some kisses for dessert.

Bring a romantic fantasy to life. Look online for local
listings under "Horse Rentals and Riding." Make
arrangements to rent one or two horses.

Go for a ride together along the beach or in the
woods. Pick wild flowers and present them to your
loved one. Spread out a blanket and have a picnic.
Spend the day riding or relaxing. Perhaps you can
finish this perfect day by riding together into the
sunset.

A Picnic to Remember

1   smartphone, computer or electronic tablet with
    Wi-Fi access
1   Internet search engine
1   limousine
1   gourmet picnic
2   sets of eating utensils and glasses
2   folding chairs
1   card table and tablecloth
1   book of matches
1   candelabra or two candleholders
Candles
Snacks

Have a first-class picnic. Hire a limousine for two or
more hours as a surprise.

Check online for local limousine services. Let your
loved one know only a few details, such as when to
be ready and what type of clothes to wear, fancy or
casual. When the limousine arrives, load the picnic
items into the trunk. Bring some snacks for the ride.
Ask the chauffeur to drive you to a park,
mountainside picnic spot or other romantic location.
Then enjoy your picnic in style. End the evening
with coffee in a romantic café, dancing or a view of
the city lights.

Option: Instead of hiring a limousine, rent a car your
loved one has wanted to test-drive.

Alone at Last

Web sites, guidebooks, travel magazines or a travel
   agent
1   reservation at a unique lodge, cottage or castle

When the two of you want to escape from the
world, rent a place where you can do just that.
Select a unique location for a getaway. For example,
stay in a lighthouse, tropical island villa, mountain
log cabin or possibly a castle in Europe.

Choose a destination that fits your tastes, budget and
offers the amenities you want. It may be a place
where you can take long walks together, cuddle in
front of a large stone fireplace, go swimming at
midnight or dance by the seashore.

On the Web or at your local library, look in
guidebooks and travel magazines or sites for
information about unique destinations and
accommodations. Also, a travel agent may be of
great help with recommendations and arrangements
for your getaway.

Best Seats in the House

2 special event tickets
1 event related item (CD, poster or jacket)
1 card and envelope
1 pen
Advance arrangements with event management

Treat yourselves to the best seats in the house to watch your loved one's favorite sporting event or performance.

Purchase tickets for seats behind the players' bench at a basketball game, in a private balcony at an opera or in the front row at a concert. Add a memorable touch to the event by obtaining backstage passes or arranging to have your loved one meet his or her favorite player.

In the card, tell your loved one that he or she is the best and deserves the best seats in the house. Attach the card and tickets to a gift related to the event, such as a CD, poster or logo jacket. One evening before dinner, deliver the surprise by placing the items on your loved one's chair.

---❤️---

Destination: Cloud Nine

Local newspaper
1   smartphone, computer or electronic tablet with Wi-Fi access
1   Internet search engine
1   hot air balloon ride for two
1   helium balloon or miniature hot air balloon
1   small card and envelope
1   pen

Arrange a hot air balloon ride for an incredibly romantic experience.

Select an FAA certified service which advertises in a local newspaper or online. Almost all flights are made at dawn. Depending upon the service's location, trips often are over valleys, farmland, hills or forests. After landing, many companies offer a champagne toast or continental breakfast.

To announce the gift, give your loved one a helium balloon with a card attached. Another idea is to hang a miniature hot air balloon ornament and card from a car's rear view mirror or on a Christmas tree. After your ride, this token will bring back fond memories of your adventure.

Dinner Date Surprise

1   romantic hotel with a restaurant
1   dinner reservation
1   hotel reservation
1   packed suitcase
1   rose
Advance arrangements with the maître d'

There is more to this dinner date than what's on the restaurant's menu.

Make dinner and room reservations at a romantic hotel. Secretly pack a suitcase for the two of you with a change of clothing, nightwear and toiletries. Stash the suitcase in the trunk of your car.

After dessert, excuse yourself from the table saying you are going to the rest room. Actually you are going to pick up two keys for the room you reserved. Arrange to have the dinner bill put on your room tab. Have the waiter deliver one of the keys to your loved one with a note to meet you in the room. Greet your loved one at the room door with a rose and a kiss.

Endless Honeymoon

1   smartphone, computer or electronic tablet with Wi-Fi access
1   Internet search engine
1   travel agent, guidebook or online service
1   reservation for the honeymoon suite at a hotel or bed and breakfast

Whether it's your first or second honeymoon, or just an opportunity for the two of you to get away, book a honeymoon suite for some serious romance.

This type of room usually has some of the facility's finest amenities, such as a private hot tub, sauna or patio. The management often provides complimentary goodies, such as a fruit basket, champagne or chocolates. You may want to hang up the Do Not Disturb sign and not leave the room at all during your romantic rendezvous.

For ideas about romantic destinations, check with your travel agent, a library's travel section or any online service featuring travel.

❧ Give your spouse a bouquet of the same type of flowers that were used in your wedding. Have the bouquet delivered to your room with a love note attached. If you don't know what the flowers were, take one of your wedding photos to a florist who will be happy to re-create the design.

Flight of Fancy

1   smartphone, computer or electronic tablet with Wi-Fi access
1   Internet search engine
1   helicopter ride for two
2   champagne glasses
1   bottle of champagne or sparkling cider
1   plate of hors d'oeuvres, caviar or chocolate dipped strawberries
1   blanket

For a date that will be cherished, arrange to have a licensed and certified helicopter service fly you to an idyllic setting on a mountain, by a lake in a valley or in a field of flowers. Helicopter services may be listed online under "Aircraft Charter."

Place the food, beverages, glasses and blanket in the trunk of your car or have these items delivered to the airport. Tell your loved one ahead of time about your plan or keep it a secret and make it a surprise.

When you arrive at your secluded destination, raise your glasses and make a toast to romance.

Flowers, Flowers Everywhere

1   smartphone, computer or electronic tablet with Wi-Fi access
1   Internet search engine
1   camera
Dozens of flowers

A gift of flowers is a special way to say, "I love you!" For an expression of your love that definitely will be noticed and never forgotten, order enough flowers to fill a room.

Find a florist through a friend's recommendation or online. Ask the florist for advice on whether to have all of the same flower or to use a variety. Order bouquets arranged in different vases and containers.

Have the flowers delivered before your loved one comes home or at a time when you know he or she will be there. It is best if you can be home when your loved one first sees the flowers. Capture his or her expression with a photo for a lasting memory.

I Did...I Do

1   religious official, ship's captain or justice of the
     peace to preside over the ceremony

It's very romantic to renew your vows. This reaffirms
your desire to share your lives together.

The type of celebration you choose will determine
the arrangements you make. Here are a few
suggestions:

- Plan the wedding you wish you could have
  afforded when you got married. If desired,
  include purchasing new rings.
- "Elope" to an exotic location, such as an island in
  the South Pacific. Before you leave, check with
  authorities to find out if you'll need to bring any
  legal papers.
- Have an intimate celebration. If you have
  children, involve them in the ceremony. Renew
  your commitment to them, as well as to each
  other.

I'd Buy You the Moon and the Stars

1   shopping spree, with some advance planning
and preparation with the store's management

Almost anyone would enjoy the opportunity to walk
into a store and be given the red-carpet treatment.
Offer to purchase anything your loved one wants
while on an extraordinary shopping trip together.

In advance, select the store(s) you want to visit. If
you do not want your loved one to know the cost of
the items, pre-select a variety from which the price
tags have been removed.

Share the excitement while watching your loved one
select the gift(s) of his or her dreams.

Invitation to an Exclusive Ball

1   hotel ballroom
1   dance band
2   catered meals
1   handwritten or laser printed invitation

Plan an evening to go dancing with your loved one. However, this night will be like no other evening of dancing he or she has ever experienced.

Secretly make plans to rent a hotel ballroom. Hire a dance band. Order drinks and a dinner that you know your loved one will enjoy. (All of these arrangements can be made through the hotel's staff.)

An invitation to this elegant evening will add a special touch. Handwrite the invitation on a blank card or design a creative invitation on a computer. Give your loved one the invitation in advance at home or when you arrive at the hotel.

As you enter the ballroom, the band will start playing your song. Dance the night away in each other's arms.

Melody Just for You

1   smartphone, computer or electronic tablet with Wi-Fi access
1   Internet search engine
1   agreement with a composer
1   CD or digital recording

Set your love to music.

Hire a musician to write a song for your loved one. To find a composer, look online for listings under "Music Arrangers and Composers." Discuss options for the song's tempo, lyrics and instrumentation. Entitle the song with your loved one's name, such as *Sara's Serenade*.

Make a recording of the song and play it during a romantic dinner. If the composer plays in a nightclub band, ask to have the song performed live for your loved one.

❤

Passionate Treasure Hunt

1	passion (or hobby) you and your loved one share
1	pen
5	to 10 small cards (3 inches x 5 inches)
5	to 10 inexpensive gifts
5	to 10 small boxes
1	pair of scissors
1	roll of wrapping paper
1	roll of tape

Have fun creating a treasure hunt and watching your loved one's expressions as the hunt proceeds. You may want to have the treasure hunt several months or even more than a year in advance of actually "delivering" the gift.

Select a passion or hobby that you both share. This could be anything from photography to mountain climbing. Decide what the ultimate gift would be for someone who enjoys this passion, keeping in mind your budget. The next page shows just two examples with three suggestions each, of varying expense.

If golf is a shared passion:
- Play the Old Course in St. Andrews, Scotland.
- Go to Palm Springs to see a PGA or LPGA event.
- Give a new set of golf clubs and take lessons together from a local pro.

If movies are your passion:
- Attend the Cannes Film Festival in France.
- Visit Hollywood, take studio tours and see the movie stars outside the Academy Awards.
- Audition to be extras in a movie. When the movie is released, go to the premiere in a limousine.

For the treasure hunt, write clues on the small cards. The clues should lead your loved one to other clues. Wrap up each clue with a small gift that will hint at the treasure. For example, give a golf tee, ball, hat, glove and shirt. The treasure may be a certificate for the golf clubs and lessons.

Hiding locations for the clues may lead your loved one around the house or to a friend's house. Consider having the treasure buried in a potted plant or the yard. When your loved one finds the treasure, enjoy sharing your passion!

Pick a Trip, Any Trip

5   travel brochures
5   envelopes, all one color or five different colors

Make a dream come true. Go to a travel agency to look at travel brochures for several destinations you and your loved one have dreamed of visiting. Check your budget and pick five destinations that are within the same price range.

Next, put one brochure into each envelope and seal. Do not label the envelopes. Surprise your loved one with the envelopes and tell him or her to pick only one. Whichever one he or she selects is the trip you'll take. Get out your calendar and start planning.

Portrait of Love

1	smartphone, computer or electronic tablet with Wi-Fi access
1	Internet search engine
1	agreement with an artist
1	sheet or large piece of cloth

Photographs of you and your loved one

A portrait of a couple in love is a lasting symbol of romance. Give your loved one a portrait of the two of you.

There are several ways you can select an artist to do your portrait. Go to art shows and galleries. Pick up the business cards or write down the names of the artists whose works you like. Also, look online for listings under "Art Instruction and Schools" or "Artists."

Choose an artist who specializes in the medium you want, such as oil, watercolor, acrylic, colored pencils or pastels. Give the artist several photographs of you and your loved one. Before commissioning the work, be sure to indicate to the artist the mood or image you envision.

Stage an unveiling of the portrait. You may want it to be a private event so your loved one can show his or her appreciation without feeling self-conscious.

Sail Away With Me

1   smartphone, computer or electronic tablet with
     Wi-Fi access
1   Internet search engine
1   sailboat or yacht
Captain and crew (optional)

Set your sails for the high seas on "your own"
sailboat or yacht. If you know how to sail, arrange
for a boat that fits your needs. If you don't know
how to sail or don't want to do any of the work,
many charters provide a captain and crew. The crew
will do all of the charting, cooking and cleaning.

Check online for listings under "Boat Renting and
Leasing," "Boat-Charter" or "Travel Agencies." You
determine the course and length of the voyage. Then
enjoy one another's company as the world
disappears at sea.

Timeless Carriage Ride

1   winter resort brochure
1   smartphone, computer or electronic tablet with
     Wi-Fi access
1   Internet search engine
1   horse drawn sleigh or carriage
1   nightclub or café

One of the most romantic rides is on a horse drawn sleigh in winter. On your excursion through the snow, bundle up and snuggle in. Sleigh rides may be arranged through winter resorts or winter resort hotels.

It also is romantic to take a carriage ride through the city to see the sights by day or lights at night. Many carriage companies offer rides year-round. These may be listed online under "Carriages" or "Carriage Ride."

After your ride, stop off at a cozy nightclub or café for an aperitif or specialty drink. Gaze into one another's eyes and enjoy being together.

---❤---

True Tale of Romance

1   smartphone, computer or electronic tablet with Wi-Fi access
1   Internet search engine
1   agreement with a writer
1   fancy photo album
1   paper punch
1   pair of scissors
1   roll of wrapping paper
1   roll of tape
Photographs of you and your loved one

See your own romantic story in print. Hire a local writer to create a story based on your romance, with the two of you as the main characters. Find a writer through a college English department or online under the keyword "Writers."

Purchase a fancy photo album that is bound in leather, velvet or a cover you like. Remove the album sheets. Use a paper punch to prepare the book's pages for the binding rings. To "illustrate" the book, select a few photos of your times together that follow the story line. Insert the photographs into the photo album sheets and place them in between pages that match the story line. Wrap up the book and give it to your loved one.

Whisked Away for Dinner

1   travel agent or guidebook
1   smartphone, computer or electronic tablet with Wi-Fi access
1   Internet search engine
1   restaurant reservation
1   hotel reservation
2   airline tickets
2   packed suitcases

The next time you feel like going out for dinner and want to make the evening memorable, try *really* authentic food. If you are in the mood for Chinese food, go to Chinatown in San Francisco. Have French food in the French Quarter of New Orleans. For Italian food, try a small café in New York's Little Italy.

It's best to plan this dinner date when the two of you can take a few days off to enjoy the cuisine and the city. You may choose to tell your loved one about the date or have it be a surprise. If it is going to be a surprise, pack a suitcase for him or her.

To find a restaurant and hotel that suit your tastes and budget, consult with a travel agent, check several Web sites or a guidebook for recommendations.

A Dash of Hints

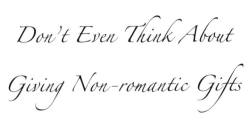

Don't Even Think About

Giving Non-romantic Gifts

on Romantic Occasions!

Appliances
Automotive supplies or equipment
Business attire
Business supplies or equipment
Cleaning supplies
Socks
Tools
Yard and garden supplies

If you are looking for a romantic gift, avoid items such as those listed above that represent work or chores. Although these may be items that your loved one needs or enjoys, they won't start any flames of passion.

Remember, for romantic occasions, purchase or make gifts that say, "I love you." There are dozens of ideas for romantic gifts in this book.

Emergency Romance Cards

6   cards for various occasions

The next time you are near a card shop, take a look inside. Purchase six cards for a variety of future occasions, such as an anniversary and birthday. Also, buy some "thinking of you" cards or "just because I love you" cards. This way, you'll never be without a card when you are inspired to share a romantic thought.

It's the Little Things That Count

2   sheets of paper (8 ½ inches x 11 inches)
1   pen

Make a list of all the day-to-day chores you can think of. Select six chores that you usually do and six that your loved one usually does. Combine the lists. Promise to do the chores together during the next month.

To add some fun, try doing the chores with a romantic twist. Here are some examples:

- Fold laundry by candlelight.
- Pay a one kiss toll for every pan or dish washed.
- Vacuum floors while dancing the tango.
- Sing a duet while making the bed.

Love on a Budget

Discount coupon or dining books
Coupons in newspapers
Coupons from visitors' bureaus

Purchase a money-saving coupon book from a local nonprofit organization, school or distributor. These books often include discounts for entertainment, lodging, restaurants, services and products. (Many are available in electronic and/or printed formats.) Also, check newspapers and visitors' bureaus for promotional discount coupons. Sources such as these may give you ideas for romantic activities, as well as save you money.

New Year's Romance Resolution

1   or 2 sheets of paper (8 ½ inches x 11 inches)
1   or 2 pens
1   or 2 envelopes

On New Year's Eve, commit to a year of romance.

Write a romantic New Year's resolution. You may choose to write this together or separately. Indicate how you'd like to express your love throughout the year. Put the resolution in an envelope. Place it in a drawer where you'll find it one year later.

Open the resolution envelope on the following New Year's Eve. Reminisce about your year of romance. Plan and commit to your next romantic year together.

Photos on the Go

1   smartphone or tablet computer with a built-in
    camera
1   single-use (disposable) camera

Smartphones and other devices with cameras are
great to capture romantic moments happen when
you least expect it.

But sometimes the device's battery is low or dead at
inconvenient times. Though, it may seem a bit old-
fashioned, a single-use camera can be extremely
useful. These cameras vary in the number of
exposures. Some have built-in flashes. Others are
waterproof for use in a swimming pool or while
snorkeling. Just slip one into your purse, pocket or
car's glove compartment. Now you'll be ready to
snap great photos while on all of your romantic
escapades regardless if your smartphone is charged
or not.

Piggy Bank Dates

1   piggy bank or jar
Loose change

If you find yourself low on cash for dates, try making an extra effort to save some money for romance.

Place your spare change in a special piggy bank or jar. The money in this piggy bank will help pay for spur-of-the-moment dates. Anytime you find a coin in a parking lot, in between the sofa cushions or in a pair of jeans before they're washed, put it in this bank, too.

How much you save may determine how creative you need to be with your dates. If you have $7, you could rent a movie and buy some popcorn. However, if you have only $1.07, your date could be a trip to the grocery store to buy a candy bar you both like. As you eat the candy bar, you each could reminisce about your childhood and favorite candy you ate as a child.

Romance Calendar

1   personal calendar
1   pen
1   package of heart-shaped stickers
Local newspaper
Local arts organizations' brochures or Web sites

When you receive or purchase a calendar for the coming year, circle or put a heart sticker on important dates, such as anniversaries, birthdays or random days you'd like to do something romantic. Schedule simple or elaborate romantic dates throughout the year.

Contact local arts organizations for information about series they'll be presenting, such as concerts, plays or art exhibitions. You may be able to find free or inexpensive series sponsored by local businesses or the parks bureau. Plan to attend the series that most interests you. These pre-planned dates are great for those with hectic schedules who need help deciding when to take time out.

❧ Make your scheduled romantic dates as much of a priority as other appointments and events.

What Do You Want to Do?

1   sheet of ruled notebook paper
1   pen

How many times have you asked your loved one, "What do you want to do?" He or she replied, "I don't know. What do you want to do?"

To prevent this dilemma, make a list of 50 activities you'd like to do together. These are activities that you think would be fun to try or have tried but rarely do.

Couples often get into the rut of doing the same things over and over, making their lives seem monotonous. Whenever the two of you find yourselves in the situation of wanting to do something different, refer to this list and pick something fun.

❧ Keep this list near your romance piggy bank or romance calendar.

When Inspiration Strikes,
File It Under "R" for Romance

1   notebook
1   pen
1   file folder or file box or
1   smartphone, electronic tablet or computer with Wi-Fi access

Start a personal collection of romantic recipes.

You and your loved one may want to keep separate romance files so the ideas can be used as surprises and gifts. In this case, use a secret file folder or box to store notes, clippings or brochures.

Clip and file advertisements for unique vacations, picturesque places to visit, special restaurants or fun activities. Collect brochures and articles about romantic places to go and things to do.

Excellent ideas also may be found online. Use a search engine by typing in key words such as romantic, romance, restaurant, picnic, dating or other words related to the information you want. Create a folder on your computer, electronic tablet or smartphone to save these ideas or Web site addresses for these future dates.

Romantic Recipe Index

This index has been designed to help you locate specific recipes. Its entries also indicate the approximate cost and complexity of each recipe. Cost and complexity may depend on personal taste and where you live.

Each recipe's cost is based on the price of the ingredient(s). The following is a guide to estimated costs noted in the next.

□ = Low = Less than $30

◱ = Medium = $30 - $100

■ = High = Over $100

The complexity of a recipe refers to the amount of time and effort it could require to create or arrange. The following is a guide that estimates the complexity of recipes based on a comparison to each other.

□ = Low = requires little effort to create or arrange. Suggested ingredients are probably readily available.

◱ = Medium = requires extra creativity or effort to arrange. Hard to find or numerous ingredients may be necessary.

■ = High = requires considerable thought and effort to create or arrange.

Legend: ☐ = Low, ◼ = Medium, ■ = High

Epicurean Delights

Legend: ☐ = Low, ◪ = Medium, ■ = High

Five-Star Specialties

	Page	Cost	Complexity
A Chapter From a Romance Novel	96	▣	▣
A Picnic to Remember	97	■	■
Alone at Last	98	■	▣
Best Seats in the House	99	■	■
Destination: Cloud Nine	100	■	☐
Dinner Date Surprise	101	■	■
Endless Honeymoon	102	■	☐
Flight of Fancy	103	■	▣
Flowers, Flowers, Everywhere	104	■	☐
I Did...I Do	105	■	■
I'd Buy You the Moon and the Stars	106	■	▣
Invitation to an Exclusive Ball	107	■	■
Melody Just for You	108	■	▣
Passionate Treasure Hunt	109	■	■
Pick a Trip, Any Trip	111	■	▣
Portrait of Love	112	■	▣
Sail Away With Me	113	■	■
Timeless Carriage Ride	114	▣	☐
True Tale of Romance	115	■	▣
Whisked Away for Dinner	116	■	■

Legend: ☐ = Low, ▣ = Medium, ■ = High

A Dash of Hints

About the Authors

We're two hopeless romantics who've been married more than 30 years. This book contains a collection of our favorite recipes for romance. We wrote *Gourmet Romance* because we believe that being romantic isn't just something reserved for special occasions.

You may have noticed that we encourage all types of getaways to keep a romance going. These can be as short and inexpensive as *A Trip to Nowhere* or as extravagant as *Pick a Trip, Any Trip*.

Please check out our travel Web site www.imaginexxus.com which features our series *A Picture Is Worth 1,000 Characters*™. This unique collection isn't a set of guidebooks. Instead they're filled with stories that are exactly 1,000 characters long and paired with original photography. Our goal is to provide readers with something that few travel books offer—a real sense of place—and in a way, take you there even before you've left home.

57668965R00078

Made in the USA
San Bernardino, CA
22 November 2017